HISTORY IN DEPTH

MEDICINE IN THE MEDIEVAL WORLD

M.V. Lyons

Head of History, King Edward VI School,
Morpeth

M

Macmillan Education

First published 1984
Reprinted 1985, 1986

Published by
MACMILLAN EDUCATION LTD
Houndmills, Basingstoke, Hampshire RG21 2XS
and London
Companies and representatives
throughout the world

Printed in Hong Kong

British Library Cataloguing in Publication Data
Lyons, M.V.
   Medicine in the medieval world.—(History in depth).
   1. Medicine—History
   I. Title.   II. Series.
   610'.9   R133.5
   ISBN 0-333-35102-9

CONTENTS

Acknowledgements

The author and publishers wish to acknowledge the following photograph sources:

Bayer Staatsbibliothek, Munchen p 42 bottom; Biblioteca Apostolica, Vaticana p 12 bottom; Bib Interuniversitaire De Montpellier pp 33 top, 47 top; Bib Medicea Laurenziana, Firenze/Photo Guido Sansoni pp 41, 43 bottom, 51; Bib Nationale, Paris pp 21, 25, 48, 50; Bib Royale, Bruxelles p 39; Bodleian Library p 42 top; BBC Hulton Picture Library p 6; British Library p 7 bottom Sloane 56 84ᵛ, p 15, p 31 Cott TIB A vii 40, p 37 Ado 17280 280 3788, p 47 bottom Sloane 2839 iv, p 53 Sloane 1977 7; British Museum p 10; By permission of the Syndics of Cambridge University Library p 33 centre; Corpus Christi College, Cambridge p 40 centre; Glasgow University Library p 14; Mansell Collection pp 5 top, 20 top, 52; courtesy of the New York Academy of Medicine Library p 20 bottom; Osterreichische National Bibliothek p 33 bottom; Photolabs — Royal Observatory, Edinburgh p 40 top; Sachsische Landesbibliothek, Dresden pp 20 centre, 43 top;

permission of the President & Fellows of St. John's College, Oxford p 46; University of Exeter — Exeter Cathedral Library p 7 top; Wellcome Institute Lib London p 45; Zentralbibliothek, Zurich p 34.

The author and publishers wish to thank the following who have kindly given permission for the use of copyright material:

Basil Blackwell for an extract from *They Saw it Happen* by W.O. Hassall; Harrap Limited for an extract from *Ibn Sina* by M. Yapp (Harrap World History Programme); The Kent State University Press for extracts from *Medieval Woman's Guide to Health* by Beryl Rowland; Peter Owen Ltd for extracts from *Medieval and Renaissance Medicine* by B.L. Gordon.

The publishers have made every effort to trace copyright holders, but if they have inadvertently overlooked any they will be pleased to make the necessary arrangements at the first opportunity.

PREFACE

The study of history is exciting, whether in a good story well told, a mystery solved by the judicious unravelling of clues, or a study of the men, women and children, whose fears and ambitions, successes and tragedies make up the collective memory of mankind.

This series aims to reveal this excitement to pupils through a set of topic books on important historical subjects from the Middle Ages to the present day. Each book contains four main elements: a narrative and descriptive text, lively and relevant illustrations, extracts of contemporary evidence, and questions for further thought and work. Involvement in these elements should provide an adventure which will bring the past to life in the imagination of the pupil.

Each book is also designed to develop the knowledge, skills and concepts so essential to a pupil's growth. It provides a wide, varying introduction to the evidence available on each topic. In handling this evidence, pupils will increase their understanding of basic historical concepts like causation and change, as well as of more advanced ideas like revolution and democracy. In addition, their use of basic study skills will be complemented by more sophisticated historical skills such as the detection of bias and the formulation of opinion.

The intended audience for the series is pupils of eleven to sixteen years: it is expected that the earlier topics will be introduced in the first three years of secondary school, while the nineteenth and twentieth century topics are directed towards first examinations.

1 THE MEDIEVAL DOCTOR

Chaucer's 'doctor of physic'. He is examining a flask of urine

A case investigation

The rider at the front of the party stretched and yawned, happy that this particular April day was a fine one. He turned in his saddle to congratulate the man who had just finished talking. Yes, it had been a good story. One or two of the ladies had even shed a tear! The doctor had told his tale well and it was now up to the leader, or host, to express his thanks on behalf of all the travellers.

Of course, it had been a good plan right from the beginning. The journey from London to Canterbury on horseback was a long, uncomfortable one. The host had decided that each member of the group should tell a story to pass the time. A good tale could take a person's mind off the dust, the stench and those devilish flies!

The host paused a moment to think about the latest storyteller. The doctor could be expected to have kept the group's attention. After all, an educated man like him should know many a good tale. 'I think he ought to do another turn on the way back,' muttered the host gruffly.

Geoffrey Chaucer

This scene has been brought to us from the imagination of a writer called Geoffrey Chaucer. He wrote a book called *The Canterbury Tales*, in the years between 1386 and 1400. He died in October 1400 before his masterpiece was complete. However, he left us not only a work of art, but also an important source-book for the history of his times.

Geoffrey Chaucer (c.1340–1400)

Chaucer probably used models for many of his characters. This means he wrote his descriptions of the travellers with real people in mind. We think this is true of the doctor. It will certainly help us to know more about medieval doctors if we can find out whether Chaucer did use a model, and if so, who this was. We are helped by the fact that Geoffrey Chaucer was a very observant man. He was able to pick out good and bad points in a person's character.

Chaucer lived in London, which was certainly the fashionable centre of England in the Middle Ages. Any doctor wishing to make a name for himself would probably have to work for a time in London. There were three physicians, or doctors, of the fourteenth century who stood out amongst all others as the most famous and the most important. These were the 'three Johns':

John of Gaddesden (1280–1361); John of Arderne (1307–80); John of Mirfield (died 1407).

Chaucer's model is likely to have been one of these three.

Chaucer's comments and observations about his doctor can help us to choose between the three possible models. It is now your task to examine the clues and try to uncover the identity of Chaucer's doctor.

Who was the model for Chaucer's doctor?

One of Chaucer's first statements seems at first reading to be very complimentary:

> *No one alive could talk as well as he did on points of medicine and surgery.*

This is a very grand claim. Of all the doctors in the world, this one knew most about his subject. Or could the statement have another meaning? Was Chaucer paying a great compliment or did he intend to suggest something completely different? Is it possible that he was suggesting that the doctor thought he knew better than anyone else?

The poet also tells us that the physician was interested in astronomy, which is the study of the planets and stars. We are told that, 'He watched his patient's favourable star'. He used the stars to forecast the health and treatment of his clients. He also used magic charms to help him cure people.

Another version of Chaucer's doctor from a late 15th century manuscript

One part of the doctor's character was particularly disliked by Chaucer. He tells us that the physician would work closely with the chemists of the time to squeeze as much money as possible from his patients. The doctor was very secretive about his earnings:

And kept the gold he won in pestilences.
Gold stimulates the heart or so we're told.
He therefore had a special love of gold.

Chaucer's doctor was well-dressed too, 'in blood-red garments'.

Chaucer has left us four important clues about the character of his doctor. Read the brief character descriptions which follow and try to identify any similarities with Chaucer's physician.

John of Gaddesden

John of Gaddesden

He was not a modest man and he claimed that his book, *The Rose of Medicine*, was better than anything written on the subject. Gaddesden seems to have been particularly interested in making a great deal of money. A later writer had this to say of Gaddesden's greed:

He has such a respect for the wealthy that he is always preparing the most select and expensive medicines for them, and if they are very rich he orders twice the quantity for them as he does for the poor.

Nevertheless, Gaddesden had a good reputation and was appointed as one of the King's doctors. Like most doctors at this time, he was interested in magic and astronomy. Some of his cures might seem strange to us. For loss of memory he recommended eating the heart of a nightingale. A person who had a history of fits was told to take cuckoo meat mixed with pig's bladder and mistletoe.

Gaddesden claimed to have cured the King's son of smallpox. He did this by dressing the boy in red materials and changing all the floor-coverings and curtains to red.

John of Arderne

John of Arderne

He was a surgeon, and in the fourteenth century surgeons were often looked upon as less important and less skilled than doctors. However, he was popular amongst the doctors of his time and well-respected by them. John of Arderne was a fairly modest man. We learn from his book that he wrote about his failures as well as his successes.

Arderne was also concerned with making money. He wrote that a surgeon should make a clear agreement with his patient about the fee. This should be taken in advance. A rich person eager to be cured should be charged a high fee. However, Arderne also insisted that a surgeon should 'sometimes give of his earnings to the poor'.

There is nothing to suggest that John of Arderne was an unpleasant person. His book contains advice on how doctors or surgeons ought to behave. For example he tells the surgeon, 'always to put God first in all his doings'. He also believed in the value of astronomy.

John of Mirfield

This doctor criticised the behaviour of many of his fellow-physicians. In his book, written in 1380, he was particularly angry:

> *Modern doctors possess three special qualifications and these are to be able to lie without being caught out, to pretend to be honest and to cause death without feeling guilty.*

Mirfield believed that very few physicians were good Christians. He complained bitterly about the dishonesty of some doctors. He said some would even prolong a patient's illness to make more money. John believed that nature was the best healer and much more likely to work than the cures of doctors. He was perhaps the most serious-minded of the 'three Johns'.

Like the other two, however, Mirfield believed in the power of magic and astronomy. He also thought that patients should not be told to give up all pleasures to cure their illness. A cheerful, comfortable patient was more likely to get well.

Questions

1 What do you think are the four clues which Chaucer provides about the character of his physician?
2 Can you eliminate any of the three 'suspects'? If so, give your reasons.
3 Which do you think is the more likely model for Chaucer's doctor? Explain your decision by referring to Chaucer's evidence.
4 Can we be absolutely certain that any one of these doctors served as Chaucer's model? Give reasons for your answer.
5 The case investigation has already provided us with some ideas about the motives of medieval doctors. One doctor's motives for doing his job might be different from another's.

motives: reasons for doing something

   Write about the motives of John of Arderne. Consider the following questions which will help you.
   a Beliefs: did he think his work was of benefit to people?
   b Money: was he concerned with making a good living?
   c Status: did he want to be seen as a successful, important person?
   Do you think he had any other motives?

The case investigation may have helped you to see that not all doctors at this time had the same ideas, practices and standards of behaviour. However, it is not possible to make such a detailed study of *every* physician and surgeon to see how they carried out their tasks from day to day. Sometimes in history we must try to make people and events less complicated by finding out what they had in common. If *most* doctors believed that the stars and planets were helpful, we can state that *in general*, doctors believed this was so. Historians call this *generalisation*.

It is important that we know a practice or belief was very common before we *generalise*. It is also advisable to indicate that even where 'most people believed this', or 'many people practised that', we make sure that we write words like 'many' or 'most'. Usually we would not wish to write 'all', except in very unusual circumstances.

You will notice that words like 'most', 'many', 'some', 'few', and so on, occur very often in this book. It would help if you understood that this is one way to avoid generalisations which are not accurate.

'The workers in this art': who were the doctors?

In the first part of the Middle Ages, most of the doctors in England were probably monks. These were men who lived apart from ordinary people in monasteries. They gave their lives to the worship of God. Monks had to obey strict rules and spend a great deal of time in prayer.

The duties of some monks included the care of people who were sick or had a disease. A young man who entered a monastery might have learned medicine along with his other subjects. We know from writings of the eleventh century that monks were certainly practising as doctors. Many monasteries had an infirmary, which was a place for the infirm or sick. Nuns also worked in these infirmaries, under the supervision of the monk in charge.

The monasteries were also places of learning and education. They usually contained a small library and a writing room or 'scriptorium'. Few ordinary people in the Middle Ages could read or write. Copies of medical books were kept in many monasteries throughout Europe.

In the medieval world, the kind of medical attention people received depended upon who they were. A rich person like a king or a nobleman would have had better medical treatment than a poor person. This does not mean that the poor had no one at all to whom they could turn.

The king's doctor

Medieval English kings had their personal physician who supervised the monarch's health and medical treatment. This man was *medicus regis*, which is a Latin phrase meaning 'The king's doctor'. The king would pay his physician and the amounts that were paid would be written on to a roll of parchment. Often, the records of these payments are all the evidence we have about the king's medical adviser. An unbroken line of royal doctors can be traced in this way as far back as the time of Edward the Confessor (1042–66).

A little more information can be found from the reign of Henry II,

A coin (back and front views), minted by Thomas of Weseham, surgeon to Henry III

(1154–89). In the records of Henry's time we are told that one of his physicians, Master Ralph de Bellomont, was drowned in the English Channel in 1170. Henry de Saxeby was one of the doctors concerned with the health of Henry III. He was given the title of Serjeant Surgeon to the king, and this office has been preserved to this very day.

Master Thomas of Weseham, a surgeon in the king's service, was so well regarded by his royal master that he was even allowed to mint coins. This privilege was usually held only by the king himself.

When the infant Henry VI was taken to France at the age of nine months, he was accompanied by a staff of surgeons. His advisers wrote this note to the young baby:

> *May it please your Majesty . . . on the advice of your council to order that four surgeons take residence in your household under the charge of William Stalworth, and to have sixpence a day each. In addition a grant to be made of twenty pounds for medicines, instruments, dressings and other necessities for your use and the use of your followers in your present journey.*

Medicine for the common people

Ordinary people would not have employed a personal doctor. It is likely that most of the sick or diseased would seek help from the local monastery or even the parish priest, who, if he did not have a great knowledge of medicine, could at least call upon God's help to relieve the suffering of the unfortunate villager.

In most villages there would be an old person who knew something about traditional remedies or medicines. These were usually passed down by word of mouth, though some had been written in books called 'leechdoms'. 'Leech' was an Anglo-Saxon word which meant healer. The 'leechdom' was a book of remedies used by the leech. Some of these remedies would seem very strange to us, and you will learn about some of them in chapter 3.

Cures could be sought too in the markets and fairs which could regularly be found in the villages and towns. There would often be a self-styled 'doctor' who had no training or qualifications, but claimed to know much about the art of healing. He could probably mix old herbal remedies, mend dislocated limbs, perhaps even set a fracture in splints. He might also pull out an aching tooth. Look at the picture opposite which shows a barber surgeon ready to demonstrate his dental skill at the Friday Fair.

Villagers might also seek out the local 'wise woman' who could attend to a variety of ailments, from the charming of warts to the curing of fits or fainting attacks. Unfortunately 'white witches', who were thought to use supernatural powers to do good, were often accused of black magic if things went wrong. The penalties of such witchcraft were extremely severe and 'proven' witches could be drowned or burned or simply put to death by an angry mob.

The majority of people dealing in medicine and healing amongst ordinary people were not professional physicians who were trained and qualified. As schools of medicine were set up in major European centres (see chapter 2), the number of specialist doctors increased. In England, despite a lack of medical schools, the number of physicians increased and by the fourteenth century it would not be unusual for a townsman to visit a 'doctor of Physik'.

The qualifications of a medieval doctor

Physicians were expected to have particular qualifications necessary in their dealings with the sick. We learn about these from books written by physicians or medical teachers during the later Middle Ages. One writer, called Isidore, who lived in the Spanish city of Seville, introduces us to certain subjects which a medieval doctor might need to know:

> *The Doctor is commanded to know* grammar, *in order to be able to understand and repeat what he reads. Similarly he must know how to* speak and write well *so that he can explain properly the diseases he treats. As well as this he must be able to use* logic and reason *to investigate and cure the causes of infirmities.* Arithmetic *also, so that he can count the number of hours in pain.*

A physician and his assistant from a 13th century manuscript. What do you think they are doing?

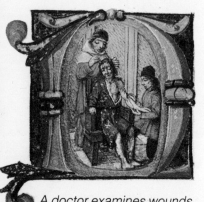

A doctor examines wounds, helped by his assistant. What is this picture contained in?

Not satisfied with these four qualities, Isidore claims that physicians should also have some familiarity with three subjects which we would probably not associate with our doctors:

> In the same way geometry, *because of the different areas of the body and the situation of parts he ought to observe. As well as this,* music *will be known to him, for music can be of great benefit to the sick. Lastly, he will know* astronomy, *so that he can study the stars and the seasons, for as a famous physician says, our bodies change as do the planets and stars.*

It is generally accepted that doctors today are well qualified and, we hope, well trained. It would seem that their medieval counterparts were also expected to have reached a high standard of education and instruction. Gui de Chauliac adds further demands in his *History of Surgery*, written in 1363:

> *The conditions required of a surgeon are four: the first is that he be educated; the second, that he be skilled; the third, that he be ingenious; the fourth, that he be well behaved.*

In his book Chauliac draws up a list of many other things a physician or surgeon should study, including 'things natural, non-natural and unnatural':

> *The doctor must have good memory, good judgement, good motives, good presence, and sound understanding, and that he be well formed, for example, that he have slender fingers, hands steady and not trembling, clear eyes etc.*

A medieval doctor's code of behaviour

Doctors were expected to behave in such a way that they would not bring disgrace or disrepute to their profession. Many medical authors at this time indicated in their books the kind of things a physician should or should not do. Here is a brief summary of these ideas, many of which are taken from a book of John of Arderne, written in about 1376.

A medieval physician should:

Always put God first in all his doings.

Sometimes give of his earnings to the poor.

Abstain from much speech, especially among great men.

Avoid the company of knaves and dishonest persons.

Always be occupied in things that apply to his craft, whether reading, studying, writing or praying.

Have excuses ready for not being able to take a case ... he could pretend to be hurt or ill.

Be courteous at the lord's table, and not displease the guests sitting by either in word or deed.

Hear many things but speak only few.

If the patient or his friends and servants asks how long the cure will take, the surgeon had better always say twice as long as he really thinks.

Always be soberly dressed.

Have clean hands and well shaped nails, free from blackness and dirt.

In strange places he should be content with the meats and drinks which he finds there.

A medieval physician should not:

Be found rash or boastful.

Laugh or joke too much.

Get drunk, 'for drunkenness destroys all wisdom and brings it to nothing'.

Annoy servants, but rather to try to gain their love and their goodwill.

Be too rough or too familiar, but adjust his manner to the character of the person; to some respectful, to some friendly.

Tell a lie, for if he be found truthful in his speech, few or none will lack confidence in his deeds.

Look too boldly at the lady or the daughters or other fair women in great men's houses, nor offer to kiss them.

Make any definite diagnosis of any illness unless he has first seen the sickness and the signs of it.

Betray accidentally the confidences of his patients, either men or women, nor belittle one to another, even if he should have cause.

Walk too quickly.

Show his instruments to the patient.

Fight or brawl in the patient's house.

Criticise fellow physicians.

Fees

Many physicians were criticised for the size of the fees they took, and it was not uncommon for patients to try to avoid paying for treatment. As you have seen, Chaucer's 'doctor of physik' was anxious to make a good living from his practice. John of Arderne had advice concerning fees and how they should be estimated:

If he does undertake a case, he should make a clear agreement about payment and take the money in advance ... And if he sees that the patient is eager for the cure, then the surgeon must boldly adjust his fee

Doctors attend to a patient. Does the appearance of the physicians seem to confirm the evidence concerning their fees?

to the man's status in life. But the surgeon should always beware of asking too little, for this is bad both for the market and the patient.

A modern author writing about the fourteenth century tells us that:

. . . doctors were persons of important status. They wore belts of silver thread, embroidered gloves and donned golden spurs when they rode to their visits attended by a servant. Their wives were permitted greater expenditure on clothes than other women, perhaps in recognition of the large fees doctors could command.

It is possible that the writer may have found some evidence for this statement in the works of Giovanni Boccaccio, who composed a collection of tales about a group of Italian people who were escaping from the great plague of the fourteenth century. In his book, Boccaccio tells of an aged doctor:

Although he had reached extreme old age, he married a beautiful and noble girl of his city, whom he kept supplied with rich clothes and jewels and everything which could please a woman, beyond any other woman in the town.

John of Mirfield insisted that physicians should consider their duty to attend to the poor, and to administer treatment to poor people with as much care and thoroughness as to their richer patients. Though many doctors probably agreed with him, there were also many others who wished to line their pockets with the large fees from more wealthy patients.

Women in medicine

During the Middle Ages, women were often excluded from activities and professions which were open to men. It may surprise you to learn that in an age when women could not become secretaries, teachers, lawyers, or hold other responsible positions, we have evidence that some women did become doctors, often in the face of hostility from men.

As early as the eleventh century, women are known to have practised medicine, notably at the famous school of Salerno. One of the most outstanding of these ladies was called Trotula, and she is thought to have written important works on the diseases of women and the care of children. Later medical experts, usually men, denied her existence and said that the books which bore her name were the works of other, male doctors.

We learn from one source that:

> ... *in the fourteenth and fifteenth centuries, women doctors did practise in the city [Salerno]. Women do, in fact, seem to have been tolerated in medical practice as in no other profession. One reason for such tolerance is that caring for the sick was regarded as charity and came within the scope of those who were in orders, nuns as well as monks.*

It is natural of course, that women should be associated with the practice of midwifery, or assistants at childbirth. Examine the picture which shows a midwife with her charges. Men were usually content to permit women to deal with midwifery and diseases largely connected with women and children. Where women seemed to threaten to break into the ranks of professional doctors, they were met with hostility and suspicion. One such case came to the public's attention in France in the fifteenth century. A woman was brought to trial for practising medicine without being properly qualified.

A birthroom scene

The following pages contain an imaginative reconstruction of that trial. The general story is true and most of the witnesses were actually present. The first four witnesses for the prosecution were *not* present at the trial. They have been included only to demonstrate what some famous male doctors thought of women physicians.

The Trial of Jacoba Felicie

A Paris courtroom in 1322. The room was quiet and only a few murmurs greeted the entry of the accused woman, Jacoba Felicie. There were more people present at court than usual, for this case was most uncommon and curiosity had drawn many who would not normally have attended.

The courtroom was arranged in the usual style for this type of case. The clerk of the court, seated at a table in the centre of the green-tiled floor, was busy making a few final notes. The witnesses were silent and thoughtful and only the spectators, as was to be expected, made any real noise.

The judge, Lord John of Paris, entered in his usual self-important manner, followed by four men who were there to provide him with legal advice. The people stood in respect as John entered.

Clerk Be seated! The accused will come forward.

John of Paris Who brings the complaint?

The Dean of Medicine I do, my lord. On behalf of the University of Paris Medical Department. I accuse the woman, Jacoba Felicie, of practising medicine without proper qualifications, and without a license from the authorities.

John of Paris How does the accused plead?

Jacoba Not guilty, my lord.

John of Paris Let the trial proceed. Bring on the witnesses.

There is a buzz of interest around the room as some of the most eminent doctors of the time prepare to give their evidence. The first witnesses are those for the prosecution. They are hostile to women who practise medicine and also to those who are unqualified and do not have a license.

The Prosecution witnesses

Gui de Chauliac Women and many ignorant people entrust the sick, with all kinds of diseases, to the care of the Saints. They rely on this saying: 'God has given as he pleases and God shall take back as he pleases!'

John of Mirfield Worthless women are taking over our profession for themselves and they use it wrongly. They have no natural ability nor proper knowledge. They make the greatest mistakes thanks to their stupidity, and very often kill their patients.

John of Arderne   I know of one patient who was under treatment from a so-called healer who was, in fact, an unqualified woman. Needless to say the treatment was unsuccessful, even after half a year.

Arnold of Villanova   In my third book I dealt with the treatment of sicknesses which particularly concern women, and as women are in general poisonous animals, my next book will deal with the bite of poisonous creatures!

The Dean of Medicine   The accused has practised and continues to practise medicine in Paris. She has never qualified to practise and does not possess a license from any official place of study at Paris or any other medical school.

The Defence witnesses

Jean Faber (Patient)   I was suffering from a sickness in my head and ears at a time when it was very hot. Jacoba visited me and showed great care and concern. I was cured from my illness by the medicines she gave me and by the help of God.

Lord Odo (Patient)   I was seized by a severe illness, to such an extent that my own limbs could not support me. Jacoba visited me both at the hospital and at the public baths where I went for cure. She and her helper, Master Jean, gave me a purgative [medicine to clear away the harmful matter which was thought to cause illness]. They prepared medical baths for me and treated me with ointments and bandages. They took such good care of me that I was completely restored to health.

Jeanne Bilbaut (Patient)   I had been seized with a fever and very many doctors had visited me to try to cure me. I was not even able to speak and these doctors gave me up for dead. And so I would have been if Jacoba had not come at my request. She worked so hard to heal me that with God's help I was cured.

Finally, Jacoba herself is called to defend her actions to the court.

Jacoba Felicie   It is more proper for a woman to attend other women, especially if the healer is clever and expert in the art of medicine. Some women may be embarrassed by having to go to a man for a cure. I have proved my ability to cure and heal the sick. Many qualified doctors have tried and failed to heal certain patients whom I have later cured. Surely it is better that I am allowed to make visits and give treatment than that the patients die through the failures of licensed physicians?

The verdict

Jacoba was found guilty and excommunicated (expelled from the Church), and forbidden to practise medicine.

Before you are too hard on the medical masters of Paris, do not forget that Jacoba was on trial for practising without a license, not simply because she was a woman.

Questions

1 'Biased' means one-sided. A person who is biased only accepts his or her own side of an argument or point of view.
   Is there any evidence of bias among the prosecution witnesses? Explain your answer.

2 Arnold of Villanova is particularly harsh on women, and not just women doctors! What is his argument against women? Does it make sense to you?

3 What can you say about all the Prosecution witnesses? What do all the Defence witnesses have in common?

4 Jacoba argued in court that *experience* (i.e. practice and observation) was more important than paper qualifications (i.e. training and schooling), in the practice of medicine. Do you agree? Explain with reference *only* to this case.

5 You have already examined the motives of John of Arderne (page 7). What do you think were the motives of Jacoba Felicie? Is there any difference between the two sets of motives? Explain by referring to the evidence.

6 The picture on page 11, showing a barber-surgeon waiting to pull teeth, is an *imaginative reconstruction*. This means that the artist who drew the picture had to use his imagination, together with the evidence available to him, to try to reconstruct the scene as though he was there. We call this empathy. The important thing for the artist is not to let his imagination work without the evidence. Both are essential. What kinds of evidence would *you* want to examine if you were asked to draw such a scene? Examine the picture carefully and make a list, with explanations, of the sources of evidence you would need.

'THE TREE OF PROGRESS'

When we talk of 'progress' we mean advancing to a higher stage. In simple terms, progress means improvement. The historian or student of history is interested in how and why improvements happen. This is true of the history of medicine because there are many reasons why progress is made.

One reason for progress in medicine is that people learn from others who have worked and studied before them. Ideas are passed on through writings, inventions, equipment, and so on.

Another way in which progress is made, is that people learn from their contemporaries, those who live and work at the same time, perhaps in different parts of the world.

We may use the diagram below to show how ideas spread and helped to improve some practices in medieval medicine. The roots of

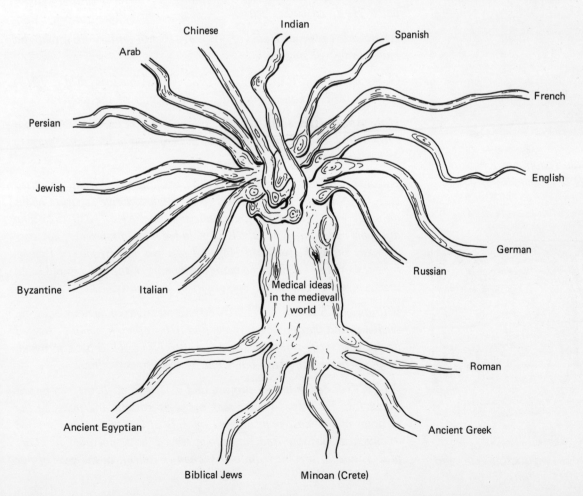

Hippocrates, 'the father of medicine'

Galen examines a flask of urine. (The picture was drawn in the 15th century, long after Galen's death)

Rhazes, 'the prince of practising doctors'. He lived in Persia (Iran)

the tree are the ideas of people before the medieval period. The branches show the races of people in the medieval world who contributed to the progress that was made. You will learn about their achievements in this chapter.

Medieval physicians relied very much on the writings of 'masters of medicine' who had lived in what historians call Ancient times. This age included the civilisations of the Ancient Greeks and later the Romans.

Below you will find a number of extracts from a book written by the French surgeon, Gui de Chauliac, which will show you how previous 'masters' of the medical art were thought to have contributed to medical progress:

The first of all was Hippocrates (fifth century BC), who outshone all the others, and first among the Greeks shed new light on medicine. He lived ninety-five years and wrote many books on surgery.

Galen (second century AD) followed him, and what Hippocrates wrote, he practised and improved. He wrote many books in which he included much about surgery, containing wounds and ulcers and boils. He lived eighty years.

After Galen we find Paul (of Aegina, seventh century AD), who did many things in surgery.

Going on we find Rhazes (died c. 923 AD), Albucasis (died c. 1013) and Alcaran. Rhazes collected all the sayings of the ancients.

Haly Abbas (late tenth century, was a great master . . . Avicenna (980–1037 AD) followed him, and in very good order treated surgery in his fourth book.

Roger (of Salerno, practised c. 1170), Roland (of Parma, practised c. 1200), and the Four Masters (anonymous), wrote separate books on surgery . . . Then we find Jamerius (worked c. 1230–52) who did some rude surgery in which he included a lot of nonsense; however in many things he followed Roger. Later we find Bruno (of Longoburgo, worked c. 1252) who made a summary of the findings of Galen and Avicenna and of the operations of Albucasis.

William of Saliceto (c. 1210–80) wrote two collections, one on medicine and the other on surgery; and in my opinion, what he treated he did very well. Lanfranc (died c. 1306) also wrote a book in which he put scarcely anything but what he took from William.

And I, Gui de Chauliac, surgeon and master in medicine . . . doctor to our lord the Pope, I have seen many operations and many of the writings of the masters mentioned, mainly of Galen . . . and studied as much as possible and for a long time I have operated in many places, and at present I am in Avignon (France), in the year of our Lord 1363.

Gui de Chauliac, the great French surgeon

Questions

1 Chauliac seems to be suggesting a *line of surgeon/doctors* through whom progress has been made. He suggests a *continuity*. Make a note of all the statements and phrases you find in these extracts which indicate that some doctors copied, followed or borrowed from others.

2 Does Gui de Chauliac seem to criticise this state of affairs? Explain your answer.

3 Construct a time line which covers the period 400 to 1500 AD. Select a suitable scale (e.g. 2 cms = 100 years). Your scale will depend upon the size of your paper.

   Mark on to your line the doctors and surgeons of the Middle Ages. (You will not be able to include Hippocrates and Galen, who lived before that time.)

   Whenever you read of other doctors or persons who contributed to medical ideas, write them on to your chart. You may wish to include the 'three Johns' for instance.

   As your chart develops, you could add some drawings or symbols to illustrate the information. Examples can be found in this book, and you will find more in a library.

You may conclude from de Chauliac's writings that medieval physicians were aware of the work of their predecessors, the doctors who lived and practised up to a thousand years before them. Not only were they aware of these people, but to a large extent relied upon them for much of their medical knowledge.

De Chauliac was a devoted follower of the teachings and practices of Galen. In this he was like many of his fellow physicians in the Middle Ages. Yet Gui was able to criticise some of his contemporary physicians (i.e. those who lived and worked at the same time as himself), because he believed they merely followed customary ideas:

I do not know whether it is from fear or love that they scorn to hear anything except what is traditional or proved by authority.

He has some advice for these people:

Let them believe the teaching of Galen ... which is entirely based on experience and reason, in which one seeks things and not mere words ... Galen also refers to witnesses as a third argument to use with experience and reason.

Gui de Chauliac sums up the beliefs of many medieval doctors when he writes:

... he who would know something better than the others, must suddenly be very different from the others ... he must be seized with a

21

certain love for the truth; he must not cease to study day and night, to learn all that has been said by the most famous of the ancients.

In general, the medieval physician did not seek a real understanding of the causes, symptoms and treatment of disease. His main aim was to collect and study the opinions of the 'ancient masters' about a particular case and use this as the basis for his actions.

Meeting places of medieval medicine

A physician working in England would probably wish to learn of any remedies or surgical practices that had been used successfully in another part of Europe, or indeed, outside Europe. He could do this either by reading about new ideas or by talking to visitors from abroad who may have known about them.

The main channels of such ideas and practices were the land and sea trade routes which are shown on the map. As traders, merchants and travellers passed along these routes, they would bring new ideas and methods with them. This is particularly true of medicine, because there was a profit to be made from new herbal remedies, drugs, equipment and even books containing details of ideas and practices. We know that all these things circulated. This will be how Gui de Chauliac obtained copies of the books he mentions in his *History of Surgery*.

Sea and land trade routes of the Middle Ages

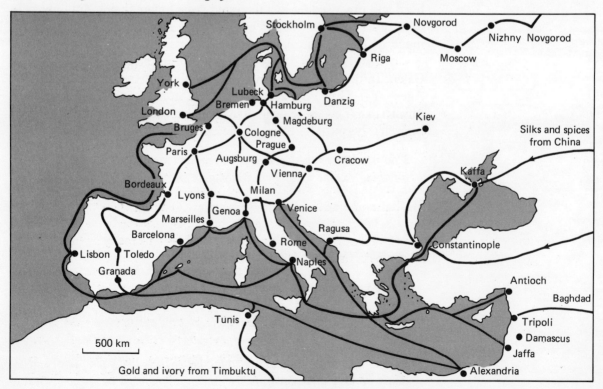

A good example of trade and ideas passing along the same routes is found in the fourteenth century. The Chinese, who had a vast number of remedies and medicines, traded with Europe. The principal commodity was silk, but with it the Chinese introduced some of their remedies, notably rhubarb!

Ideas and practical advice came from other areas as well, like the lands of the Arabs, and Persia (modern Iran). Indian medicine also found its way to the Arabs and from them into Europe.

Until the end of the fifth century AD, much of Europe and North Africa was controlled by the Romans. For many reasons the empire of the Romans gradually became smaller and many of its former territories were occupied by invading groups. Areas which we now know as Spain, France, parts of Italy and England, were settled by the peoples whose descendants are still there today. France, for example, was settled by the Franks; England by the Angles, Saxons, Jutes and others.

Arab medicine

While Europe was involved in this great upheaval, a new force had come into being in the area we now call the Middle East. Islam, the religion and way of life which had been launched by the prophet Mohammed, was carried into vast areas by the invasions and conquests of the Arab peoples.

In their libraries and 'Houses of Wisdom', the Arabs collected much of the medical knowledge which had been built up from the days of Hipprocates. Baghdad became a centre of learning.

The Arab physicians, like their European counterparts, were convinced that the writings of the 'ancient masters' were still of unquestionable value. Avicenna (real name Abu Ali al Husain ibn Abdallah ibn Sina), wrote a collection of medical books called *The Canon of Medicine*. Even this great master often repeated the opinions of Hippocrates and Galen.

Though many Arab doctors depended on the advice of Hippocrates and Galen, there was a certain element of new thinking in Arab medicine. Avicenna obviously believed in using the evidence before him, though he too would hear nothing against the 'ancient masters'. His observations on the human pulse are as true today as they were in Avicenna's time:

> *By studying the irregularities of the pulse it may be possible to discover the identity of the loved one, if the patient will not reveal it. This is done by repeating any names while keeping the finger on the pulse. When it becomes very irregular and almost ceases, one should repeat the process. I have tried this method repeatedly, and have discovered the name of the loved one. Then in the same way, mention the streets,*

dwellings, arts, crafts, families and countries, joining each one with the name of the beloved, and all the time feeling the pulse, so that when it alters on the mention of any one thing several times, you will infer from this all particulars about the loved one as regards name, appearance and occupation.

The Arab influence reveals itself most of all in the field of pharmacy, or the preparation of drugs. The Arabs had a large collection of remedies, many of which are still used today. Avicenna was perhaps mainly a chemist and used a certain preparation for the treatment of gout, which was very advanced indeed and is still in use today.

You have already seen examples of how literary evidence can be of great value to students of history. Literary evidence is gained from books and writings which are not usually of a historical nature, but are more likely to be of an imaginative, non-factual character. *The Canterbury Tales* is such a work, as is *The Decameron* of Boccaccio; both of them were used in chapter 1.

You may have heard of a famous book called *The Arabian Nights*. The real name of this book is *Alf-Lailat wa Laila* or *The One Thousand and One Nights*. This is a group of many stories which, it is thought, were finally put together into a collection in the thirteenth century AD. One story tells us a great deal about medieval Arabic ideas concerning health and medicine.

A slave girl was about to be sold by her master, who had wasted his fortune and was in great need of money. The girl was very clever and in no time at all a wealthy buyer was found. However, before he was prepared to pay the asking price, he wanted to make sure she was as clever as he had been told. He had her questioned by experts, one of whom was a skilled doctor.

The extracts which follow are the answers which Tawaddud, the slave girl, gave to the physician. They tell us a great deal about what the Arabs knew of the human body (anatomy), the main organs of the body, symptoms of disease and cures, diets, and many other things. As many of these ideas were gained from Galen, there is a close relationship between Arab and western European ideas:

The human head
There were created for him [man] seven doors in his head, which are the eyes, the ears, the nostrils and the mouth … The eyes were given the sight sense, the mouth the taste sense and the tongue to speak what is in the heart of man.

The organs and senses
Moreover, Allah [God] made him a heart and spleen and lungs and six intestines and a liver and two kidneys and buttocks and brain and bones and skin and five senses: hearing, seeing, smell, taste, touch.

gout: a disease which attacks the joints, causing pain and swelling

spleen: an organ situated near the heart which serves to produce certain changes in the blood
intestines: channels leading from the stomach as part of the digestive system

24

ventilators: fans to refresh
and cool the body
corrupt: rotten, impure
unsound

jaundice: a condition caused
by obstruction of the bile,
(fluid produced by the liver),
in turn causing yellowness of
the skin and other symptoms

*Moreover, Allah hath appointed the tongue as interpreter for the
thought, the eyes to serve as lanterns, the nostrils to smell with, and
the hands for grasping. The liver is the seat of pity, the spleen of
laughter and the kidneys of craft; the lungs are ventilators, the
stomach the store-house and the heart the prop and pillar of the body.
When the heart is sound, the whole body is sound, and when the heart
is corrupt, the whole body is corrupt.*

The symptoms or signs of illness
*A physician who is a man of understanding, looketh into the state of
the body and is guided by the feel of the hands, according as they be
firm or flabby, hot or cool, moist or dry. Internal disorders are also
shown by outside symptoms, such as yellowness of the white of the
eyes, which suggests jaundice, and the bending back, which suggest
disease of the lungs.*

Diet
*He who would live long, let him be early with the morning meal and
not late with the evening meal ... and let him make of his belly
three parts, one for food, one for drink and the third for air ... as
Galen says, 'who will take in food, let him go slowly and he shall not
go wrongly'. The stomach is the house of disease, and diet is the basis
of healing.*

Question
Several imaginative books have been mentioned in chapters 1 and
2; Chaucer's *Canterbury Tales*, Boccaccio's *Decameron* and *The
One Thousand and One Nights* written by many Arab authors.
Poets, novelists and storytellers can provide us with valuable
historical evidence, but can you think of any reasons why literary
evidence may not *always* be of great value to a historian?

India and China

Indian surgeons were highly skilled and could undertake many
operations which European surgeons may have avoided. An example
of this was a technique of skin grafting known as 'Indian grafting'
which is still used to this day. After about 1000 AD, Indian medicine
gradually merged with that of the Arabs, as trade links between the
two developed.

The Chinese, like the Indians and the Arabs, knew a great number
of remedies and medicines based upon the use of plants and drugs.
Opium, for example, was used as an anaesthetic, and arsenic for skin
diseases. The Chinese also practised the science of acupuncture in the
Middle Ages, using golden or silver needles. These were inserted in a

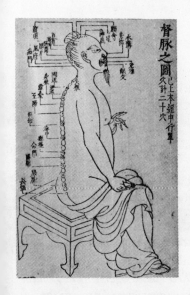

*A Chinese drawing showing
some acupuncture points*

pattern at certain points in the body, as shown in the picture, either to sensitise or influence these important points or to make areas of the body numb whilst the doctor operated. Acupuncture is still practised today, and the western world has learnt from the Chinese example. The famous medieval explorer Marco Polo spent much time in India and China between 1271 and 1275 AD. On the map you will find some of the comments he made on his journey about the medical practices of the areas he visited:

The medical observations of Marco Polo

Tabriz   *In this province there is a monastery called St Barsamo. The monks weave woollen girdles which they afterwards lay on the altar of St Barsamo ... they give some of them to their friends and to noble men because they are effective in relieving the body of pain.*

Tabriz

Badakhstan   *On the mountain tops the air is so pure ... that if a man falls sick of a fever, he has only to go up into the mountains, and a few days' rest will banish the malady and restore him to health.*

Mysore (Lar)   *These Brahmans live longer than anyone else in the world. This is due to their very light feeding and great abstinence. They have very good teeth, thanks to a herb they are accustomed to eat, which is a great aid to digestion and is very good for the human body ... these Brahmans do not practice any form of blood letting.*

They take quicksilver and sulphur and mix them together and make a drink of them, which they then drink ... They drink this mixture twice a month from childhood in order to live longer. And certainly those who live to such a great age are addicted to this drink.

Mys

Qu

Quilon   *They have no lack of skilled astrologers. They have physicians who are adept at preserving the human body in health.*

26

Khan Balik *The kings and all the dukes, marquises and counts, barons, knights, astrologers, physicians, falconers and many other officials and rulers of men and lands and armies appear before the Khan in the great hall.*

It is thronged with multitudes from all parts. His whole household staff is here with him, besides physicians and astrologers and falconers and other officials in great numbers.

Khan Balik

Kinsai *In the other streets are established the doctors and astrologers, who also teach reading and writing.*

. . . if they come across some poor man by day who is unable to work on account of illness, they have him taken to one of the hospitals of which there are great numbers throughout the city.

Manzi *Among them there are wise philosophers and natural physicians with a great knowledge of nature.*

Karajang, Vochan and Yachi *There are no physicians. When someone falls ill he sends for the magicians, that is the cunjurors of devils.*

Maabar *The body of Saint Thomas lies in the province of Maabar. When anyone falls sick . . . they give them a little of this [churchyard] earth to drink. No sooner has he drunk than he is cured.*

Basman

Basman *When one of them, male or female, falls sick the family send for the magicians to find out whether the patient is due to recover.*

Questions
Examine the writings of Marco Polo. Find one example of each of the following aspects of health and medicine in the East:
a   diet
b   medicines or drugs
c   superstition (Christian)
d   superstition (non-Christian)
e   astrology
f   the important status (position) of doctors

Medical education and training

The teachings of the 'ancient masters' together with ideas gained from Arab, Jewish, Indian and Chinese physicians, formed the basis of the knowledge of European doctors and surgeons in the Middle Ages. If this knowledge and experience were to be shared and passed on, there had to be centres where students and teachers could meet. It was during the thirteenth and fourteenth centuries that many of the universities which were to provide these centres were founded. Most of the new universities had a faculty or department of medicine. However, even before the universities were formally opened, schools of medicine existed in some parts of Europe, notably Spain, Italy and France.

By the twelfth century, seven schools of medicine had been set up in Italy alone, but it is in Spain that the real breakthrough probably began. The southern part of Spain had been invaded by the Arabs as part of the great thrust of Islam. Four of the great cities occupied and improved by the Arabs were Granada, Toledo, Cordova and Seville. Cordova became known as the 'Baghdad of the West'.

Study and learning were encouraged by the Arab caliphs (leaders) and the science of medicine in particular was stimulated. Many Jewish

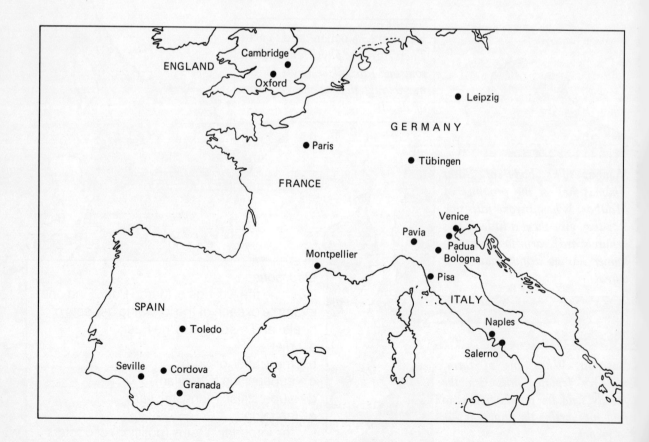

people had settled in Spain before the coming of the Arabs, and they too were anxious to record and spread their medical knowledge. Arabs, Jews and Christians worked together in Spain at the centres of learning set up by the caliphs. The map shows the principal schools of medicine and universities which had important medical departments.

Italy was in a good position to become a centre of learning. As a peninsula situated in the middle of the busy Mediterranean trade-routes, it received both the wares and the ideas of its trading partners. Salerno became the most important school of medicine in the eleventh century and remained so for some time, until the school at Montpellier in France surpassed it.

There were several ways to become a doctor licensed to practise medicine. A hopeful student had to achieve at least a Bachelor of Medicine degree or, even better, a Doctor of Medicine degree. Before starting a medicine degree, most students were first required to have a Bachelor of Arts (BA) degree, or a Master of Arts (MA) degree. This in itself could take three to four years. Usually the process of becoming a qualified and licensed doctor took at least eight years.

Below you will find examples of two courses followed in German universities at the end of the fifteenth century.

1 Tubingen

Time	Year 1	Year 2	Year 3
8 am	Galen's *The Art of Medicine*	First book of Avicenna	*The Sayings of Hippocrates*
1 pm	Avicenna's *Book of Fevers*	Ninth book of Rhazes	Galen

2 University of Leipzig

Time	Year 1	Year 2	Year 3
6–7 am	First book of Avicenna with explanations	Galen with explanations	*The Sayings of Hippocrates* with comments
1 pm	Ninth book of Rhazes with commentary	Further books of Avicenna	Further books of Avicenna with comments
3 pm	During this time the doctors read various works aloud, especially the *Book of Symptoms* of Hippocrates.		

As you can see the courses are very much fixed on the study of previous masters of medicine. Many of the lectures were on the *theory* of medicine, that is, ideas and beliefs about medicine. In some universites, like Oxford, it was possible for a fully qualified doctor to leave having never had contact with a patient!

The teaching consisted mainly of lectures, reading of books and disputations (discussions or debates). It seems that courses had much more to do with talking and listening than with any practical experience for the students. An English priest called John of Salisbury (fifteenth century) declared:

The young people pride themselves on their knowledge of Hippocrates and Galen, make use of unfamiliar expressions and introduce their sayings on every occasion.

Some universities, like Bologna in Italy and Montpellier in France, did allow the teachers to dissect, or cut up human corpses, to gain knowledge of the anatomy, or structure, of the human body.

Many universities were controlled by the church authorities and, as you will see later, the Church did not approve of dissections.

Questions

1 Gui de Chauliac seems to be contradicting himself on page 21. Can you see how?
2 Find examples from the chapter of how medical ideas and practices were spread by the following:
   a conquest or invasion
   b trade
   c exploration
   d study
   Use the examples to explain how all four were important.
4 Many historians have suggested that the Middle Ages was a sterile or unproductive period for ideas, learning and science. They say that medieval people introduced few new ideas and that old ideas were imitated. Considering *only* the field of medicine, from what you have read in chapter 2, would you say that little or no progress had been made? Or do you think some advances are apparent? Explain your answer with examples.
3 How do the medical courses offered at Tubingen and Leipzig demonstrate medieval doctors' reliance on 'ancient masters'?

The picture here acted as a grim reminder to its medieval audience. The bearded miser gloats over his treasure whilst behind him Death, the grinning skeleton, opens his coffin. The message is simple: do not think too much of worldly things for death is never very far away.

This reminder was all too realistic to someone living at this time. For the majority of people, life was hard and conditions were bad. We have no accurate records of the average age of death, but from the evidence we have we know that life expectancy (that is, how long the average person could expect to live) was very low compared to ours.

There were many kinds of diseases and illnesses in the Middle Ages which we have now eradicated. Epidemics also were more frequent. Leprosy, for example, was widespread in England. Many leper hospitals were founded throughout the country. People who suffered from this disease found silvery scales formed on their skin, and the affected parts were gradually eaten away. You will learn more about lepers in chapter 4.

Below you will find a list of some of the illnesses or diseases which were common but of which we do not see much today:

Scurvy   a disease caused by lack of fresh fruit and vegetables. Weakness, tenderness of gums, foul breath, aching limbs.

Bubonic plague   'The Black Death', carried by the fleas which lived on the black rat. Brought to Europe on trading ships. Frequently fatal.

Scrofula   also called 'The King's Evil'. Extreme swelling of glands. It was believed that the monarch could cure this by laying hands on the affected person.

Sweating sickness   a fever in which the victim would suffer extreme fits of sweating. It was often fatal and epidemics were common in the fifteenth century.

St Anthony's Fire   a terrible rash which constricted (squeezed) the blood vessels and could result in the loss of a limb.

Dysentery   a disease of the bowels and large intestine which caused stomach pains and diarrhoea. It was often fatal.

St Vitus's Dance   chorea – the 'dancing madness' which spread in the fifteenth century from Germany. The affected person suffered violent shaking and movement of the muscles, which looked like dancing.

St Pernel's Disease   better known as ague. A malaria-type fever marked by fits of hot and cold sweating.

St Erasmus's Disease   another name for colic – severe attacks of pain in the stomach due to an infection in the bowels or other parts.

Pellagra   also known to medieval people as St Aman's disease. Probably caused by eating infected maize. Skin reddens, dries and cracks. The digestive organs and nervous system are affected. The disease often ended in insanity.

As you can see, many diseases were named after saints. This was because medieval people believed that saints could both inflict and cure these diseases. Measles, for example, became known as St Lazarus' disease. The list shows only some of the 'pestilences' or diseases from which people suffered at this time. There were, of course, hundreds more which threatened medieval people.

Scrofula – 'The King's Evil': a case study

The pictures opposite show the ideas and practices of medieval physicians in trying to deal with one of the complaints, scrofula. Examine the pictures carefully and read the instructions which accompany them.

1 *There are three types of scrofulas, those in the throat, those under the shoulder joint and those in the groin ... When they come to a head, cut them ... so that the pus [yellowish discharge] comes out. If they harden and swell for a month or six months, or if the patient is a boy, use this oil ... [a prescription is given]. At the declining of the moon, make eleven poultices [hot, soft mixtures] of iris and wild radish; use one on the tenth day, another on the ninth, and so on to the end of the moon. On this, or some other day, bleed him once. If this medication is not sufficient, surgery must be resorted to ... the patient's throat should be firmly held with one hand while the outer skin is cut, then scraped and the scrofula caught with a hook and drawn out.* Fourteenth century manuscript, Roger of Salerno

2 *For scrofula tumours and boils: use the herb scelerata softened and mixed with pig dung into a dough; apply to the scrofula tumours and boils and within a few hours it will waste them and the pus will disappear.* Thirteenth century manuscript from Vienna

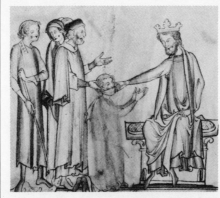

3 *Kings can cure this disease.* King Edward the Confessor lays hands on a scrofula victim. From a thirteenth-century manuscript

The evidence gives us some clues about the ways in which medieval physicians could and did treat sickness. Consider the words below and read the explanations which accompany them:

Surgery medical treatment by operation. Treating disorder by operation.

Medicine to heal or cure by medical means; to administer preparations for the relief of disease.

Magic/superstition belief in the power of the unknown. Based on fear or ignorance.

Purges ridding the body of excess or harmful impurities. The clearing of excess substances.

Questions

Using these explanations, find one example of each of these practices from the evidence provided concerning scrofula.

Why do you think *all four* methods were suggested as possible remedies for the disease?

The 'four humours'

In order to treat sickness and disease it is necessary to understand, or at least think you understand, what *caused* the illness. When a modern doctor prescribes a medicine, he or she will know which of the causes the medicine is supposed to cure. In our own time we believe that these causes of illness are the germs or viruses of a particular disease.

Medieval people knew nothing of germs. The physicians could not develop medicines to attack germs because they did not know that germs existed. What then, we must ask, did physicians believe was the cause of disease?

Examine the pictures carefully. They show four moods or 'humours'. Most medieval physicians believed that these 'humours'

had to be present in the body in equal balance if good health was to be achieved. If you had too much or too little of one or another of them, ill-health resulted. This belief was based on the theories or ideas of ancient philosophers (thinkers). Greek philosophers had worked out that there were:

FOUR ELEMENTS	Air	Fire	Earth	Water
FOUR SEASONS	Spring	Summer	Autumn	Winter
WHICH WERE	Moist	Hot	Dry	Cold
SIMILARLY THERE WERE FOUR HUMOURS	Sanguine	Choleric	Melancholy	Phlegmatic
DEPENDING ON THESE LIQUIDS IN THE BODY	Blood	Yellow Bile	Black Bile	Phlegm
LEADING TO THESE HUMAN CHARACTER-ISTICS	Passionate Active Emotional	Angry Ill-Tempered	Sad Gloomy Dreamy	Unexciting Dull Even-tempered

Question

Try to match the 'humour' to the picture. Which man do you think is sanguine, for example? Which one is melancholy, choleric or phlegmatic? Explain why you have chosen each of the four.

As you know, physicians in the Middle Ages relied much on the writings of the 'ancient masters'. They accepted the idea that too much blood or black bile was dangerous to health. The obvious solution was to remove it.

If you think about it carefully, the theory of the 'four humours' has a certain logic to it. Suppose a woman has a cold. She has an excess of phlegm or mucus. She is miserable and lacking in energy. Based upon these observable symptoms, the 'humours' theory seems to fit. Use the evidence provided, to write a justification of the theory from the viewpoint of a medieval physician.

The following extracts are taken from the works of the Greek philosopher Aristotle (384–322 BC), whose ideas were believed and used by many medieval physicians:

1   *Drawing of blood was first invented for good purposes ... To bleed in the left arm removes long continued pains and headaches. It is also good for those who have got falls and bruises ... Bleeding is a most certain cure for no less than twenty-one disorders, and for many more with the help of drugs, herbs and flowers. When the moon is on the increase, you may let blood at any time, day or night; but when she is on the decline, you must bleed only in the morning.*

2   **Q.** *Why are the heads of men hairy?* **A.** *The hair is the ornament of the head, and the brain is purged of ill-humours by the growing of the hair ... it is answered that the brain is purged in three different ways; of unecessary watery humours by the eyes; of choler by the nose; and of phlegm by the hair, which is the opinion of the best physicians.*

3   **Q.** *Why is the head subject to aches and griefs?* **A.** *By reason that evil humours proceed from the stomach up to the head and disturb the brain; sometimes it proceeds from filling the stomach too much.*

4   **Q.** *Why do men sneeze?* **A.** *That the virtue and power of the sight should be purged and the brain also from unecessary matters; as the lungs are purged by coughing, so is the sight and brain by sneezing: and therefore physicians give sneezing medicine to purge the brain; such sick persons as cannot sneeze, die quickly, because it is a sign their brain is wholly stuffed with evil humours, which cannot be purged.*

5   **Q.** *Why is it wholesome [good] to vomit?* **A.** *It purges the stomach of all naughty humours, expelling them, which would breed again if they remain in it; and purges the eyes and head, clearing the brain.*

6   **Q.** *How many humours are there in a man's body?* **A.** *Four, whereof everyone has its proper place. The first is choler ... which is placed in the liver. The second is melancholy whose seat is in the spleen. The third is phlegm whose place is in the head. The fourth is blood whose place is in the heart.*

Question

Compare these statements, which most European doctors believed, with the extracts on pages 24–5 which show Arab medical beliefs. What similarities can you find, particularly on the 'four humours' and the importance of the stomach? Are there any differences?

Supernatural causes of disease

The word 'supernatural' means above nature – beyond the natural. We usually apply the word to things which mystify us, things we do not understand.

Medieval people could not always provide an explanation for the causes of disease. The 'four humours' theory seemed adequate for most cases, but many sensed that there were other causes, supernatural ones.

From the evidence we have it seems that there were three main ways in which the supernatural was thought to have an influence on both diseases and cures: religion; astrology; superstition.

Disease and death were ever-present threats to medieval people. How is death depicted in this picture?

Religion as an influence on disease

Until the beginning of the sixteenth century, there was only one main Christian religion in Europe. God was often considered to be vengeful, that is, a God who severely punished wickedness and wrongdoing. It seems that medieval people were more aware of this side of God's character than the loving, forgiving aspect which most Christians accept today.

When plague arrived in Europe, known to medieval people simply as 'the pestilence', most men and women believed that God had sent a dreadful punishment for their sins. Pope Clement VI himself, the leader of the Church, agreed in 1348 that the disaster was a 'pestilence with which God is afflicting the Christian people'. A European ruler called it 'a chastisement (punishment) from heaven'. The English poet William Langland wrote a long poem whose hero, Piers Plowman, said 'these pestilences were for pure sin'.

God is deaf now-a-days and does not hear us.
And prayers have no power the Plague to stop.

Those who believed that God had sent the plague also thought that only God could remove it.

Giovanni Boccaccio left us a very vivid description of the plague which clearly indicates how medieval people saw the hand of God:

... 1348, when into the famed city of Florence, the most beautiful town in Italy, there came the death-dealing pestilence which, through the operation of the heavenly bodies [planets] or of our own wicked dealings, being sent down upon mankind for our punishment by the just anger of God ... And here neither wisdom nor foresight nor even humble prayers, not once but many times, both in organised processions and in other ways made to God by devout persons, could prevent its horrible effects.

Many Christians believed that God would only remove the dreadful plague if the offenders showed signs of sorrow for their wickedness. Large groups of people marched from city to city, stripped to the waist, whipping each other in turn, often until blood was drawn.

One observer, an Englishman called Robert of Avesbury, described how these 'flagellants', as they were known, came to London in 1349:

About Michaelmas 1349 over six hundred men came to London from Flanders, mostly of Zeeland and Holland origin. Sometimes at St Paul's and sometimes at other points in the city they made two daily public appearances wearing cloths from the thighs to the ankle, but otherwise stripped bare. Each wore a cap marked with a red cross in front and behind. Each had in his right hand a scourge with three tails. Each tail had a knot and through the middle of it there were sometimes sharp nails fixed. They marched naked in a file one behind the other and whipped themselves with these scourges on their naked

Flagellants in procession.
Can you see the 'scourges
or whips?

and bleeding bodies. Four of them would chant in response. Three times they would all cast themselves on the ground in this sort of procession, stretching out their hands like the arms of a cross. The singing would go on and each of them in turn would step over the others and give one stroke with his scourge to the man lying under him. This went on from the first to the last until each of them had observed the ritual.

Astrology as an influence on disease

Most popular newspapers today have a column devoted to 'Your Stars'. Many of us look upon these daily forecasts as a lighthearted amusement, not to be taken too seriously. The people who write such forecasts like to be known as astrologers.

Medieval physicians took the science of astrology very seriously indeed. Most physicians carried a small book called a *Vademecum* (meaning, go with me) which helped them to remember all kinds of information they thought helpful. One section would be devoted to the stars, showing how they affected different parts of the body.

Aries   the Ram, governs the head and face
Taurus   the Bull, governs the neck
Gemini   the Twins, governs the hands and arms
Cancer   the Crab, governs the breast and stomach
Leo   the Lion, governs the back and heart
Virgo   the Virgin, governs the belly and bowels
Libra   the Balance, governs the veins and loins
Scorpio   the Scorpion, governs the groin and sexual organs
Sagittary (Sagittarius)   the Centaur, governs the thighs
Capricorn   the Goat, governs the knees
Aquarius   the Water-Bearer, governs the legs and ankles
Pisces   the Fish, governs the feet

A doctor consults his astrological tables

It was believed that operations and other forms of medical treatment should only be attempted when the planets were favourable. If you turn back to page 36, extract 1, you will find that Aristotle's advice on bleeding includes a reference to the moon.

John of Arderne also believed firmly in the power of the stars to influence medical treatment:

> *The highest astrologers ... state that a surgeon should ought not to cut or cauterize any part of the human body nor to bleed a vein so long as the moon is ruling that part. For the twelve signs of the zodiac rule the twelve parts of the human body, as is clear from the drawing. Where Aries, which is a fiery sign moderately dry, governs the head with its contents. But when the moon is in Aries, beware of operating upon the head or face and do not open one of the head veins. When the moon is in Taurus, refrain from operating upon the neck or throat and do not bleed from a vein in these parts. When the moon is in Gemini, beware of operating on the shoulders, arms or hands, and do not open a vein in those parts. ...*

On his journeys to the East, Marco Polo often made reference to physicians and astrologers in the same phrase. It is likely that a physician would consult an astrologer before he made an important decision. This was particularly true in the case of surgeons, like John of Arderne:

Superstition as an influence on disease

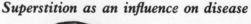

The man in the bed looks very unhappy! The bird, which is called the caladrius bird, has been placed on the patient's bed for a strange purpose. Many physicians in the Middle Ages believed that if the caladrius bird looked *at* the patient, he would recover. If the bird looked away, as in the picture, death would be the result. No wonder the patient looks dismayed. He even seems to be trying to attract the bird's attention!

Even the great Leonardo da Vinci later believed that similar powers were possessed by the goldfinch. The cockerel in the other picture also indicates the 'magic' value of birds. The patient has been bitten by a mad dog. The physician throws down grains of wheat before he treats

the wound. If the cock eats the wheat, the patient is supposed to recover.

Medieval medicine was steeped in beliefs like these. However, it would not be fair to say that physicians relied upon such ideas and excluded any scientific approaches. As you will see in the next section, medieval medicine was a mixture of scientific practices with strong currents of supernatural and superstitious influences.

Exercise

The picture shows the title-page of a book, depicting some of the ingredients which make up the great mixture of ideas and beliefs held by medieval physicians. Try to find at least one *symbol* representing each of the following aspects of medicine in the Middle Ages:

religion; evil; good; astrology; fortune (luck); science.

Doctors, surgeons and others involved in healing and medicine believed that people were somehow influenced by all the 'forces' represented in the picture. If they believed that these 'forces' contributed to *causing* illness and disease, how would this affect their attitudes to *cures* and *remedies*? Would these be influenced?

Signs and symptoms

In order to work out a cure or remedy, for a sick person, a doctor has first to find out what is causing the suffering. This is called diagnosis. Once a diagnosis has been made, the doctor might then be able to tell the patient and family how the disease is likely to develop.

Hippocrates and Galen, whom medieval physicians often attempted to imitate, had developed a system which we call 'clinical observation'. These great doctors carefully observed the patient's symptoms, noting any changes in condition. A complete history of the patient's case would be kept so that if anyone else caught the disease or illness it would be recognised.

Unfortunately, the methods of these two 'masters' had become neglected. Instead of noting *all* the symptoms and signs, doctors in the Middle Ages concentrated on one or two symptoms. The pulse and urine were regarded as the most important signs of a person's state of health.

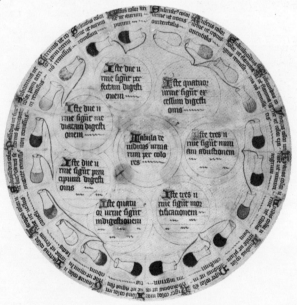

The picture shows twenty flasks, each one containing a sample of urine. The samples are each of a different colour and each flask is labelled in Latin to show the colours and the state of digestion which each colour indicates. If you turn back to page 4 you will see a physician examining a flask of urine, whilst the picture here shows an apparently conscientious doctor checking his books to make sure his diagnosis is accurate.

The reading of the pulse was equally important. Regularity, pace and force of heartbeat were noted by the able physician. Advice was given on where the pulse should be taken, the exact position of the fingers and even that the hand should not be so cold as to shock the patient.

Treatment of disease and illness

The methods employed by medieval doctors to heal their patients varied with the nature of the ailment or disease. You examined the case of scrofula earlier in the chapter. Four types of treatment appeared in the evidence: medicine; surgery; purging; a magical remedy. These then were the methods used according to the doctors' experience and knowledge about a particular illness.

Medicines and drugs

The most important branch of the art of healing was the use of medicines and drugs. These were made chiefly from herbs and animals, though some minerals were also used. Medicines were not only mixed and prescribed by doctors. Many unqualified people knew old remedies which had been passed down over the years and they would be happy to share their knowledge with a neighbour, sometimes for a reward.

Many books of medical recipes existed to which doctors and others could refer for cures. These volumes were often made up of ancient (i.e. Greek and Roman) recipes, Moslem remedies and even perhaps some traditional ideas from a particular country. In England, for example, old English 'leechdoms' existed which contained Anglo-Saxon recipes for medicines.

A typical medical book may have been divided into sections which dealt with remedies made from the following: spices, salves (ointments) and oils; animal products; plants; trees; wines and stones.

The picture shows the next stage in the process. A physician is seated (left) and giving instructions to both an assistant, who mixes the ointment, and a secretary, who writes down the prescription.

Medieval doctors had a great number of remedies to draw upon and although some of these medicines may seem strange to us, many of their ingredients are still in use today.

Remedies often combined a medical approach with a completely non-medical idea. For example the other picture shows 'The Eagle Remedy' for poor eyesight:

For dimness of vision. It is said that the eagle, when he wishes to fly high to view the nature of things, eats wild lettuce. Anoint your eyes with juice of wild lettuce and its leaves softened by honey and you will attain the maximum of clear eyesight.

Sometimes the cure appears to be completely without reason. For example, John of Arderne recommended that a patient suffering from epilepsy (a disease causing fits) should have the crumbs of roasted cuckoo blown up his nostrils!

Ideas like this have caused many people to regard medieval medical practices as primitive and backward. A deeper look into many of the remedies reveals that there were also practical and well-tried cures.

Medical recipes of the fourteenth century

A good liquid to break the catarrh in a man's head and also a cold in the head: *Take a red onion and cut it up small, and boil it in a little clary; and boil it well and add a little honey; and when they are well boiled, add a spoonful of mustard, and boil a long time. Lay the man on his back, and put a little of the mixture on his nose, and let him stand up and sneeze. Do this twice a day for three days and he will be well again.*

For loss of speech: *Take the juice of southern wood or of primrose, and he shall speak at once.*

To make a man or woman sleep three days: *Take the gall of a hare, and give it in his food, and he shall not awake until his face is washed with vinegar.*

Whoso has a perilous cough: *Take woodsage, rue, rummin, and pepper, and boil them together with honey; and eat thereof a spoonful each morning and evening; and you shall be cured.*

For heartburn: *Take a crust of a white loaf that is right brown, and eat it when you go to bed; but do not drink thereafter, and so lie and sleep all night and that shall drive the heartburn away.*

Medicine for the tertian fever that takes a man night or day: *When you think that it will take him, have a cake of barley meal made and let him eat it as hot as he can; afterwards give him plenty of good wine to drink before the ague comes on him; then take four plants of plantain with the root and cut them all up and crush them and mix the juice with a spoonful of wine and four spoonfuls of water. Let him drink before the ague comes and heal him well, and let him sleep and he shall fare well.*

rue: a strong scented evergreen shrub used for medicine

clary: a plant native to Southern Europe but grown in England as a pot herb. 'Clary water' or 'clary wine' was a medicinal drink made from clary-flowers

tertian/ague: malarial-type fevers, marked by fits of sweating

southern wood: a deciduous shrub or plant having a fragrant aromatic smell and a sour taste, much cultivated for medicinal purposes

gall: the bile (bitter fluid) from the gall bladder, a small bag on the liver

woodsage: a herb with dull yellow green flowers with a heavy aromatic smell, and a bitter flavour

plantain: a herb with broad flat leaves spread out close to the ground

Surgery

The rather miserable looking man in the manuscript illustration is a 'wound man'. We have many similar examples from the Middle Ages and these help us to assess the kind of wounds which surgeons thought they could treat. It is thought by some medical historians that the science of surgery was improving from the twelfth century:

By about 1100 definite progress was evident, a result, it seems of Arabic influences. Latin translations of the works of Rhazes, Avicenna, and of a notable surgeon named Albucasis, and experimental operations by practical-minded men in the regions of Salerno, Bologna and Montpellier, mark the dawn of Western Surgery.
L. Mackinney: *Medical Illustrations in Medieval Manuscripts*, 1965

There was a revival of interest in anatomy, the study of the structure of the body. Animals were dissected (cut up for detailed examination), and by 1300 an Italian surgeon named Mundinus was undertaking

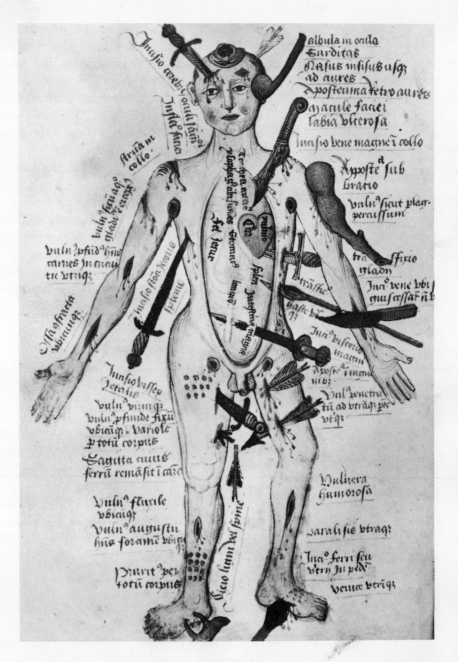

post-mortem (after-death) examinations of human bodies. Through the influence of Mundinus at Bologna University, dissection became common practice in every medical school. Public dissections (i.e. where any interested people could attend), were introduced into Montpellier in 1366, Venice in 1368, Florence in 1388 and into Germany and Eastern Europe during the fifteenth century.

Unfortunately, these dissections rarely improved the knowledge of the human body to any great degree. This was because the master in charge of the dissection would usually just read the observations of Galen, or an imitator of Galen, whilst assistants dissected the body to prove that Galen's observations were true. It rarely happened that a master would make first-hand observations of the body alone.

Warfare was very common in the Middle Ages. Local quarrels between one great Lord and another, or national disputes between rival princes or kings, often led to bloodshed. In England for example, the wars with France, which we call the Hundred Years War, had hardly finished when the disastrous Wars of the Roses began in England itself.

Although these wars brought untold misery to the various countries or areas involved, they did have one beneficial side-effect. Surgeons were able to gain invaluable experience in the treatment of wounds, the practical knowledge of anatomy and the development of methods and techniques of surgery. When an army went to war, it was invariably accompanied by physicians and surgeons.

In the tenth century, Albucasis, the great Moslem physician, could present the drawings of tools you see here to demonstrate the wide range of surgical instruments available. The list below shows the names of the instruments:

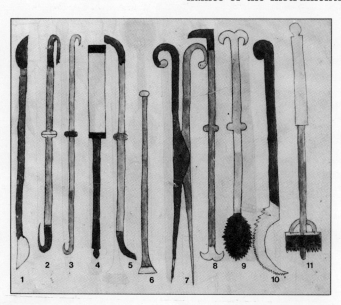

1 Scalpel
2 Hook
3 Hook
4 Probe
5 Double-ended knife
6 Skull chisel
7 Dilator for stretching (used to widen the wound for better access)
8 Knife
9 Cranial saw
10 Cranial saw (cranial = skull)
11 Trephine for boring into the brain

Questions

The surgical implements show one aspect of medieval technology i.e. practical science; equipment for a practical use – surgery. The physicians did not, however, have very advanced tools, aids and equipment. What effects might this have had upon medical progress?

The 'wound man' indicates the range or variety of operations which might be attempted. Most of them are *external*, i.e. on the surface of the body. Why do you think this is so?

Much thought was given to the problem of pain and shock in operations. Attempts were made to produce an anaesthetic which would put the patient to sleep. John of Arderne mentioned several in his writings. One suggestion was an ointment made up of mandrake plant and opium. He claimed that this would enable the surgeon to operate without the worry of a distressed patient.

The recipe below shows one suggestion for an anaesthetic:

To make a drink that men call dwale [night-shade, a sleeping-potion mentioned by Chaucer], to make a man sleep while men operate on him.

Take the gall of a boar, or, for a woman, of a spayed sow, and three spoonfuls of the juice of hemlock, and three spoonfuls of wild briony, and three spoonfuls of lettuce, and three spoonfuls of opium poppy, and three spoonfuls of henbane, and three spoonfuls of vinegar; and mix them all together and boil them a little, and put them in a glass vessel well stopped. And add three spoonfuls of this mixture to a bottle of good wine or good ale, and mix them well together ... And then let the man who is to be operated on sit by a good fire, and make him drink the potion until he falls asleep. And then men may safely operate on him. And when he has been fully served and you want him to wake, take vinegar and salt and wash well his temples and cheeks and he shall wake at once.

More often than not, patients had to be held down or tied down because an effective anaesthetic was not known. You may well imagine, for example, the pain and shock experienced by the patient shown in the picture who has evidently had part of his skull pierced without anaesthetic. Accompanying the picture was the following advice:

For mania [madness] or melancholia incise [cut] the top of the head in the shape of a cross, and perforate the cranium so as to expel the [hurtful] matter. The patient is to be held in chains and the wound healed as described.

Cauterisation

Cautery is the practice of burning a particular point on the body to prevent the spread of 'corrupt matter', i.e. harmful substances, to stop the flow of blood and to ease bodily pain. It may be done either by the use of a heated iron or by applying a burning substance like quicklime.

In the picture a doctor is about to administer the cautery iron. He is holding a jar which might contain a burning substance or a soothing ointment. The picture is labelled:

For aching head and flatulence [upset] of the breast and hands, and pains of the knees and feet, burn thus.

The practice of cauterisation was widespread and extremely painful. Charts were available to physicians which showed the points at which the cautery-iron was best applied. Many doctors were convinced that cauterisation was a highly effective treatment for all kinds of complaints.

Leeching. Can you see the leeches?

Bloodletting

Several references have already been made to the belief in 'purging' or cleansing of the body by drawing blood. There were several ways of doing this: (a) Opening a vein by cutting; (b) Cupping: placing a heated cup over a light cut to draw out a small amount of blood; (c) Leeching: applying leeches or blood-sucking worms to take blood.

Read the extracts below which are taken from medieval manuscripts:

> *In acute fevers, day or night if need be, one ought to resort to bloodletting ... For head-ache and madness open veins in the back of the neck ... For ailment of the mouth or toothache open two veins below the tongue ... [Bloodletting is] the beginning of health, it makes the mind sincere, it aids the memory, it purges the brain, it reforms the bladder, it warms the marrow, it opens the hearing, it checks tears, it removes nausea, it benefits the stomach, it invites digestion, it evokes the voice, it builds up the sense, it moves the bowels, it enriches sleep, it removes anxiety, it nourishes good health.*

It was very important that blood was let at the correct spot if the cure was to be effected.

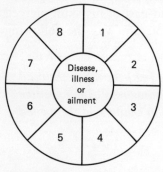

1 Symptoms?
2 Causes?
3 Diagnosis (What is wrong)?
4 Prognosis (Prediction)?
5 Supernatural aspects?
6 Medical treatment?
7 Purge recommended?
8 Surgical treatment?

Exercise

Now *be* a medieval doctor!

Copy the chart shown and insert an illness, disease or ailment of your own choosing into the centre circle. Now use your skill as a medieval physician to help your patient. In each section of your chart, fill in the relevant details. Use the evidence and information provided in chapter 2 to help you. *Remember – you must base your treatment(s) on what you believe to be the cause(s).*

Below the chart explain *why* you have decided upon the chosen course of treatment. You may wish to work with a partner who indicates his/her symptoms so that you may make your observations and decisions. Afterwards you can exchange roles.

HOSPITALS, HEALTH AND HYGIENE

The improvements that were made in medicine during the Middle Ages were often the result of the work of *individual* people. When many people work together in an organised way, with rules, regulations and a definite aim or goal, we call this an *institution*. There are many examples of institutions in the world today. A school, for example, is an institution. On a much bigger scale, charity organisations like Doctor Barnardo's or Oxfam are also institutions.

One of the most important institutions of medieval Europe was the organisation of the Christian Church. The word Church used in this way does not simply mean a building, but the whole organisation of the Christian faith. It included all those who believed in the teachings of Christ. The leader of all these people was the Pope, who lived in Rome. In each country which was Christian, there were bishops, priests, monks and nuns who helped to provide the services which Christians needed. The Church thus had a great responsibility. It also was able to suggest ideas to its millions of followers. In this way the Church had great power over its people.

The leaders of the Church were often cautious and slow to accept change. They sometimes held back ideas or practices which were suspected of being dangerous. For example most medieval people were seriously concerned about their salvation, that is, their chances of going to heaven. The church authorities prevented surgeons, or medical teachers, from dissecting human bodies. This was because they believed that men and women needed their bodies in heaven. The knowledge of the human body (anatomy) was thus held back by the Church. However, the Church did much good in the field of medicine, especially in forming hospitals.

Exercise

Consider the work of the Church from the following aspects:

a recording and preserving the medical books of the past when Europe was in an unstable period (page 9)

b providing monks and priests as doctors, nuns as nurses (pages 9, 52)

c having responsibility for education and learning in medicine (pages 28–30)

d founding and running hospitals (pages 49–52)

   How important *was* the Church to the development of medicine during the Middle Ages?

Medieval hospitals

The hospital ward in the picture was drawn at the end of the Middle Ages but it is typical of many hospitals founded in the fourteenth and fifteenth centuries. The first thing you will probably notice is the fact that it looks like the inside of a church building. There are an altar with a crucifix, areas for prayer, statues, and nuns attending to the sick. All in all, it seems evident that the Church had much to do with this particular hospital, the famous Hotel Dieu in Paris.

Before we can generalise, however, it should be noted that there were many different types of hospital in medieval Europe and not all were concerned with the welfare of the sick. The word 'hospital' comes from the Latin term *hospitalis*, which means concerned with *hospites* or guests. Some hospitals were for the use of travellers and not for sick people. However, by far the majority were set up to aid the infirm, the sick and the diseased.

More than seven hundred hospitals were founded in England between the eleventh century and the middle of the sixteenth century. By 1215 there were one hundred and fifty, and five hundred more were founded in the next two centuries. The fourteenth and fifteenth centuries together form the great age of medieval hospital-building.

There were several types of hospital in medieval England:

The infirmary   usually an essential part of a monastery, but patients were often admitted from outside the monastery.

The 'Spittle House'   hospitals for the ordinary sick.

Lazarhouses   those hospitals built only for the use of the victims of leprosy.

Maternity hospitals   of which a few had been built by the end of the fifteenth century.

Asylums   hospitals for the insane, e.g. Bedlam in London.

A typical hospital, like the one shown in the picture, was a large room divided into cubicles, with perhaps one or two private rooms.

A hospital as we know it is a place for the care, treatment and cure of the sick. Before the thirteenth century, it seems likely that hospitals were simply centres of rest where those who were ill could seek recovery in a fairly clean, quiet atmosphere.

If you examine the illustration from a fifteenth century manuscript, you will see that this small hospital certainly fits the modern definition. There are attendants waiting upon the patients. Several doctors administer treatment. The ward looks busy and efficient.

The largest hospital in medieval England was St Leonard's in York. This was built during the reign of King Stephen (1135–1154) on the site of an old Anglo-Saxon hospital. In 1370 St Leonard's housed two hundred and twenty-four sick and poor, a large establishment even by modern standards.

At St Leonard's could be found a complete staff, including bakers brewers, cooks, smiths and servants. It seems that there was a woman in charge of staff, who was perhaps the forerunner of the modern matron.

Women played an important part in the day-to-day life and running of the hospitals. Nurses were often nuns, though ordinary women were also employed (lay nurses). The position of 'matron' was probably created in the fifteenth century, when women began to play an important part in the management of larger infirmaries. The picture on the left is a woodcut from the fifteenth century, showing a lay nurse with a saucepan in her hand.

Hospitals depended to a large extent on charity for the money and supplies necessary to do the work. Church hospitals or monastic infirmaries were often financed by the Church itself. Other hospitals often had 'patrons' (i.e. a protector who looks after the interests of an individual or an institution). King Henry III was one of the patrons of St Leonard's and he allowed the hospital to collect special taxes in the surrounding counties.

The head of a hospital was called the 'master' and he was usually appointed by the patron. Masters were expected to show a high standard of behaviour and we are able to find out more about these standards from the records left by the hospital authorities of the time. Drinking and hunting were often frowned upon, and absences from the hospital had to be brief.

By the end of the twelfth century it is probable that wooden beds had replaced straw for sleeping purposes in the hospitals. Hospital records show that bedding was washed. At St Thomas' Hospital in Canterbury the warden and his wife were paid yearly for washing the beds of poor patients.

Leper hospitals

Leprosy was one of the most feared and unpleasant diseases of medieval Europe. It is still found in some parts of the world today, and people who suffer from this disease develop shining white scales on the skin. Parts of the body are slowly eaten away so that victims become horribly deformed. The disease is contagious, or catching, so you can imagine the terror which it caused to people, particularly in the towns.

To avoid contact with lepers, and to isolate them so that the disease could not spread, special hospitals were built outside towns. Near Canterbury, for example, a 'lazar-house' or leper hospital was built at Harbledown. Just outside Dover, another was built at Buckland. These were both religious hospitals, run by members of the clergy. At Buckland the leper entering the hospital had to swear this oath:

A leper rings her warning bell

I . . . , do promise before God and St Bartholomew and all saints, that to the best of my power I will be faithful and useful to the hospital, obedient to my superior and have love to my brethren and sisters. I will be sober and clean of body; and a part of the goods I shall die possessed of shall belong to the house. I will pray for the peace of the church and realm of England, and for the King and

Queen, and for the prior and convent of St Martin, and for the townsmen of Dover on sea and land, and especially for all our patrons, living and dead.

Lepers who came to this type of hospital often lived like monks, rising at all hours to recite prayers. Many leper hospitals relied on local charities. At Carlisle, for example, the lepers received a pot of ale (beer) from the local brewery each Sunday and a loaf from each of the city's bakers.

Health and hygiene

The Greeks and Romans had placed much value on the *prevention* of disease. They realised that physical fitness and hygiene i.e. keeping healthy, were essential if sickness and disease were to be avoided. The Romans introduced a very advanced public health system. This means that the authorities, the people who governed, provided the citizens of Roman towns with the conditions necessary to keep clean and healthy.

Medieval authorities, at least in England, did not accept that it was their responsibility to provide these conditions. If people wanted to be fit and clean, it was their own responsibility.

The first necessity of any public health system is a supply of fresh, clean running water. This water is used for keeping folk clean and also their clothes, food, houses, and so on. Any waste which might carry harmful matter could then be taken away by underground channels or sewers. The Romans had all these things, and more; including public baths and public lavatories.

The Romans had left Britain by the fifth century and yet a thousand years later, by the fifteenth century, medieval authorities had still not attempted to reach the high standards of public health that the Romans had introduced.

It was left to individuals or communities to organise their own water supply. This might have been a river, stream, spring or well. Many large rivers, like the Thames, were also used for disposing of waste materials. In London, it became impossible to use the Thames for drinking water because of the large amount of waste deposited.

The evidence suggests that England was particularly backward in providing health facilities for its larger towns. In Paris, a survey of 1292 indicates that the city had 26 public baths, providing either steam or hot water. The Paris authorities recognised the value of these baths as an aid to cleanliness. Each day the 'crier', a public announcer, would announce the availability of the baths:

Calling you to bathe, Messire,
And steam yourself without delay.
Our water's hot and that's no lie.

A medical bath with a physician in attendance

53

Public fountains, supplied by aquaducts, brought water to the various parts of Paris. In many French towns, public toilets existed and cesspools were dug for waste matter. Drainage pipes also existed, though open street sewers were more common, as in London. French towns employed street cleaners and carters to take waste and dirt away. Though the French system was by no means advanced, it was evidently better than the apparent lack of facilities in large English towns.

On his travels, Marco Polo noticed bathing establishments in Asia. In Kinsai (China, see map on page 27), he observed:

> ... many baths of cold water, well supplied with attendants, male and female, to look after the men and ladies who go there for a bath; for these people, from childhood upwards, are used to taking cold baths all the time, a habit which they declare to be most beneficial to good health. They also maintain in these bath-houses some rooms with hot water for the benefit of foreigners who, not being accustomed to the cold, cannot readily endure it. It is their custom to wash every day, and they will not sit down to a meal without first washing.

In the town of Kinsai alone, Marco Polo continues:

> There are fully 3 000 public baths, to which men resort for their pleasure several times a month; for they believe in keeping their bodies very clean. I assure you that they are the finest baths and the best and biggest in the world – indeed they are big enough to accommodate a hundred men or a hundred women at once.

In the province of Cathay:

> The population is so enormous and there are so many bath-houses and baths continually being heated that the wood could not possibly suffice, since there is no one who does not go to a bath-house at least three times a week and take a bath, and in winter every day, if he can manage it. And every man of rank or means has his own bathroom in his house, where he takes a bath.

In England it seems that only the houses of wealthy families and monasteries had good, private health facilities. Monasteries were models of good health practice. Most of them had very good facilities for washing, and a room called the lavatorium was reserved for this purpose.

Toilets were often situated near rivers so that sewage could be carried away. Fountains Abbey in Yorkshire had a particularly effective system. Many monasteries also had an infirmary and some even had a 'leeching house' where bleeding could be performed. Monasteries did not suffer as badly as towns and villages during the plagues, but this could be due to their isolation from centres of population as much as to their good health facilities.

Even the horrors of the first plague of 1348–9 did not seem to have much effect on sanitation in London. In 1357 steps had to be taken again to force citizens to keep their property clean. Rubbish and waste were still deposited freely into the streets, where open sewers (large gutters carrying flowing water) could not cope.

Exercises

1 Many monasteries have been destroyed since the Middle Ages, though the remains of some of them are still evident. Try to find out more about monastery infirmaries, particularly if there is a ruined monastery in your area. There are many books on medieval monasteries which are probably available at your school or in a local library. Find out where the infirmary was normally situated, its size, who looked after the sick, etc.

2 Hospital records are mentioned on page 52. Records of institutions like schools, churches, hospitals, are of great value to people who study history. Consider the kind of information we might get from hospital records. Bedding is mentioned, and payment of staff. What else would you expect to see?

3 Much of this book is based upon written sources of evidence. We can also learn a great deal about medieval medicine from non-written sources. Consider the following *types* of non-written sources:
   a   picture evidence (including maps and charts)
   b   evidence from coins, seals and medals
   c   archaeological evidence
   d   artifacts (things made by human beings, e.g. tools, weapons, jewellery, etc.)
   Write a few sentences to show how these forms of evidence might help the student of medical history. Provide examples from this book or from other sources.

INDEX